Mama Tried

Also by B. Elizabeth Beck

Fiction

Summer Tour Trilogy:
   Summer Tour
   World Gone Mad
   Under the Elm

Poetry

Interiors
insignificant
Painted Daydreams: Collection of Ekphrastic Poems

MAMA
TRIED

✿ ✿ ✿

Poetry by

B. ELIZABETH BECK

BROADSTONE

ISBN 978-1-956782-07-3

Text design by Larry W. Moore
Cover design by the author & Larry W. Moore

Broadstone Books
An Imprint of
Broadstone Media LLC
418 Ann Street
Frankfort, KY 40601-1929
BroadstoneBooks.com

Contents

EVEN YEARS LATER

I always know their flower faces,
although I do not always remember their names

would recognize them by their handwriting

can recall intimate details they once scrawled
in black ink on pages of spiral-bound notebooks

doodles, drawings, designs inscribed vertically
to the left of the pink line before the edges tatter

and corners fray. Pages torn out, impressions
left behind like ghost words too haunted to share

with a teacher.

Planning Bell

If I do not write today,
I will never write another poem

and if I never think in verse,
my window will seal shut.

So, although I should be writing
lessons and thinking about

institutionalized documents,
what I want to consider

are my children. Lost casualties
of a public education that speaks

about serving but never actually does
anything beyond talking

and talking and talking
in meetings about meetings

that swirl around my head
which reminds me

how my students must feel
loaded with words they maybe

don't understand about
content that exists in a vacuum,

much like the hum of the machines
their mamas run to suck debris

from carpets worn thread-barren in homes
that lack windows for the future when

it's enough to just survive today.

Mallory Square Sunset Festival
April 1, 2014

ain't got time to call your soul a critic, no
—Robert Hunter

I stop to reach a hand, no mistake
Warf Rat lingers from jukebox in
local bar. August West has no right
to demand help in his own demise,
when he is too drunk to stand,
yelling wounded protests on deaf ears,
other tourists do not even deem to pause.

I still stop to reach a hand, no mistake
my son watches my decision, careful
to ask permission before I retrieve black
plastic bag holding two beer cans; I am
no threat, *he is an old man down, down
by the docks of the city. I got no dime*,
but pull his weight enough to steady bare
feet on concrete so he may amble his way.

No mistake, he belongs to someone. My son
reaches his arm around mine, old enough
to bear witness as *eyes of the world*. We
turn the corner to catch his grandparents
consciously oblivious in their casual cruelty,
not stopping to ensure our safety,
even if they don't approve.

I HAVE NO POEM INSIDE ME,

I must not claim false intimacy or summon an
overheated heart glazed just in time for a camera
—Toni Morrison

no words to speak.
It's not my song to sing,
not my grief to wail,
yet if I remain silent,
I am complicit.

This poem is not
about me. It never
was. Insignificance
encased in white
skin. Willing to offer
as protection, acknowledged
as privilege in a messed-
up world. I am a mother.
Mother, teacher, woman

who collapsed, howling
screaming pain in empathy
that cuts deeper than I ever
imagined as worst fear.
It's not my worst fear

for my son's fate. Beyond
comprehensible. I would
burn the motherfucking
world to the ground. Tear
my skin from my bones.
Gnashing, snarling menace

to society, I do not
understand. This is not
my poem to write. I hold

vigil protecting my son's
spheroidal blood cells
from an unknown virus.

It never occurred to me
to worry about the cops.

And that is exactly
the problem.

For Dwayne Scott Carter, Jr.

I don't talk about you.
Instead, I named my son

Carter, even though we called
you *June*. You are not a part

of my classroom mythology.
Not accidentally. More because

your life means more than
an anecdote. Instead, I echo

your surname multiple times
a day. A breath. My son

turns his head at the beginning
consonant, C. Hard C. Car as in

unintentional ironic momentum.
You stopped. I know. Yet, I echo

your name. Honor your name.
Even as I revere Saul's war cry,

Let your children name themselves
scrawled in crayon on a scrap

of cheap public-school paper hanging
haphazardly as tape allows. I conjure

reason when floating in lavender salts
repeating circles of chaos unnecessary

yet inevitable when egos clash in order.
Chaos is what I crave. The duende tunnel

I once followed with only violet flame
to lead my way. I forgot how important

it all once was. Still is. Or perhaps
repeating your name every

time I call dinner is enough. I will
never forget. See same light shine

from brown eyes twenty years after
we bowed heads as your mama wailed

under banner classmates scrawled heart-
felt sentiments in borrowed sharpies,

I suffered sorrow yet stood
one among a crowd in church

as revered teacher. Label undeserved.

I MET GOD AT THE SPEEDWAY TODAY
—for Katya

She spoke to me. Energy into
the universe caught in ink—
chance opportunity for dreams

I have forgotten ignited in pages
of text. My heart leaps

because when you do
what you are meant, god
speaks through you.

I'm proud to remember
second person, reminded
by those who dare to howl.

When I am not silent, not
in mourning, breathe
the present, and don't worry

memory taxed by useless
words because poems
are not designed to preach

but to find truth I seek
as I listen to music and sigh.
The happily-ever-after

found in the space between
breath. Everyone thinks
but only poets write down

ideas caught as if pages
were butterfly catchers.

CASUALTIES

My job is to take care of you. I was appointed to do
that by God. —Cormac McCarthy, *The Road*

You are my son.

I feel responsible for cells
I cannot cure. Hereditary

disease flows through veins.
Blood cells misshapen lodge

in spleen. Undetected until
you were eight. Good thing,

as I would have raised
you in a bubble. Now,

I just pray.

ROUTINE

Hey, baby
I call to him each day.

I'm not a baby
he insists.

I know! Quit growing up so fast

He depends
upon this exchange
ritual in its rhythm
warmth in tone
seeks my smile
with a grin of his own.

I'm not sure
how this started
but I remember my role
meet my cues, say
my lines. When I'm
absent, he looks for
me in confusion.

Not a line I can
include in sub plans.

MOTHER'S DAY CARD ASSIGNMENT

I don't live with my mom. My mom is dead.
Don't be sad, Ms. B. I got a good granny

My mama's locked up. My mom's in Mexico.
We may go back this summer. For good. Maybe.
I have a foster mom. Does that count? I live
with my auntie. It's okay 'cept there's too many
damn kids. I sleep on the pull-out sofa. I ain't
got a room. I share a room with my two brothers.
We need a bed. Our house got burned up. Can
I go to Youth Service Center for my bag
for the weekend? I need my food. I don't need
a belt. I'll pull up my pants. Can I go to the restroom?
I just started today. *You know.* We don't have
internet at home. But I got my phone. Is this a real
rock, Ms. B? Where'd you get it? Are these
plants real? My granny grows plants. Sign my
behavior sheet please. I need all three's today.
I lost my pencil. Can I use the hand sanitizer?
Where's the hall pass? I go to grief group today.
Can you read this poem? My daddy got shot.
It's my birthday. I'm turning twelve. We go
to church on Tuesdays. And Sundays. But
mostly Tuesdays. My cast comes off next
week. My daddy gets out next month. We
came across the border. I'm not ashamed
to say it. Can I call my mom? Can I go
to my locker? Who's that in that picture,
Ms. B? Is that your son? Can I write
on the board? Can I at least erase it? Do
you have snacks? Where do you keep
your band-aids? Can I go see the nurse?
This glue stick is all dried up. Can we
use the scissors? When is this card due?

I THINK HE'S KIDDING

when he refers to Trump
as dictator. I gently
correct, *President*. His
panic is real. Believes
his father will be deported.
Understands reality better
than me. I'm too busy

remembering rushing
into classroom day after
election 2008 to use red
and blue markers on white
board. First patriotic
gesture of my life. Now
I feel deflated. Forget

to look at boy's eyes,
until he pulls on my sleeve
impatiently intent in seeking
asylum in school building.
I grant it with false reassurance
from the hours of eight to four,
he is safe. But, what about
his father? What happens

when he gets off the yellow
bus and arrives to an empty
home with a note from ICE
on the linoleum kitchen table?

That's not going to happen,
I can't say. Can't make promises.
Can only pretend I'm not worried
as I direct him to homeroom.

COMO SE DICE

Carefully copy phrases
conscious of gender articles
correctly transcribe post cards
I send to parents about my students.

I do not know enough Spanish

so I ask Spanish teacher to write
model I use to communicate.

I do not know enough Spanish.

Quickly learn, *mucho gusto* for open house.
Silencio and *siéntate* for classroom.
Quitate la gorra, por favor and
camina despascito for my duty in lobby.

I do not know enough Spanish.

Una momento, por favor flows easily
As does *mi estudiante favorito*. Finally,
te amo my favorite phrase. Like a toddler

learning to speak, my students indulge
my feeble attempts. Memorize
Shakespeare to recite in return.

I ONLY KNOW

she needs new
glasses. Do not know
it has been three years

since last eye exam. Don't
understand hesitation until
her best friend explains,

patiently, as one would
with a dimwit. As one
would with a white woman

who means well, but oblivious
to daily fear. As one who steps
from the shadows to map out

what should be obvious.
But they know I care,
and always have snacks,

so, they unravel the word,
undocumented. I nod like
it's not a surprise. Should

not be, had I paid attention.
Pretend that would not be
an issue. Prepare to pay

for new glasses myself
until social worker nods,
more experienced, reassures

me with one call to book
appointment for exam. Second
call to arrange with mother.

She returns following week
grinning behind new frames.
I do not apologize and she

does not thank me. No
need for either gesture.

RED RASPBERRIES

What are those?
I've never eaten one before.
Can I try? Why is it fuzzy?
I think it tastes sour. It's kind
of mushy. Can I have another?

Can I have a Jolly Rancher
instead? My color is blue
and not fuzzy and not mushy
and not sour. You call those
berries, *God's candy?* You're
weird, Ms. B.

HANDS UP/DON'T SHOOT
—for Tomica and Tyfini

Should not be
the call and response
her baby brothers learn
before they even
learn how to drive
but the rules
they must learn:
not to run
not to move
not to hide
not to hold Skittles
while walking black
while driving black
while living black
while being black

are rules that have
been broken
we are broken
lives are broken
hearts are broken
screams are...

Stop! I can't
breathe, he
cried, we cry,
shout, scream, mourn,
fight, rally, holler
on deaf ears our
government doesn't
want to hear, nor
do they care even
as we chant their names
calling up their spirits
holding them close

to our hearts shattered
in a breath not taken
lives stolen.

In the name of:

Emmitt Till, Trayvon Martin,
Alton Sterling, Bothom Jean,
Atiana Jefferson, Dontre Hamilton,
Eric Garner, John Crawford III,
Michael Brown, Ezell Ford,
Laquan McDonald, Akai Gurley,
Tamir Rice, Antonio Martin,
Jerame Reid, Ahmaud Arbery,
Tony McDade, Dion Johnson,
George Floyd, and Breonna Taylor

We hear you. We shout your names
into the heavens, praying your souls
are lifted as we are grounded
in an unjust world, judged by
the color of our skin and not by
the content of our character

civil rights a broken promise
Dr. King would weep tears
black brothers and sisters
and white brothers and sisters
do not sit together at the table
of justice years after he shared
his dreams deferred into shambles
Maya Angelou flies like a caged
bird freed to the top of Baldwin's
mountain where all the flowers
are the color purple, and every
black soul is free.

His Name was Angel

Opened door Thanksgiving night
for final time. His mama will
need to move away from holes
shot clear through to walls. Hard
to believe his smart mouth
caught up with him. Yet not.
Just wish it weren't true. Wish
gangs didn't bang. Fourteen
too young to die. Spoken words
cannot be erased when bullets
do the talking in response. Angelic
he does not look, gray-faced
in white casket wearing ill-
fitting suit. I don't even have
the words in Spanish for
my condolences. Look at her
hands instead of her face
creased in grief no mother
should know. Wonder if older
brother sits in church, feeling
guilt pressing down or if he
is plotting revenge. Hope
it doesn't continue. Pray
it ends here. Child in coffin.
My students wailing in pews.
Stench of death lilies. Hands
clutch rosaries. Priest stands
at attention. I do not wait
for the prayers. Push my way
past teachers lined up to pay
respect. Push front door.
Another front door. Lean
against red brick and weep.

IF THERE'S A REAL LOCK DOWN,

Ms. Beck, where will you hide us?
seventh grader asks, looking
around my yellow classroom
cheerful plants hanging in open
windows, blinds always pulled up.

I gaze at her solemn brown eyes
and gesture to corner where we
huddle for drills. But, that's not

where I will hide you if
it is real. I have a plan, dear.

No, we will not practice. It is a secret.
No one can know, but I will tell you.

We will quickly hurry into girls'
locker room. Yes, boys, too.
The outside door locks from within.
There is a second door. Look. I have
this thing I can slide to stop door.
I carry it in my purse at all times.
My husband bought it for me after—

Anyway, a shooter will have
to barge through two doors
and shoot me before he can get
to you, my students. I will stand
waiting while you huddle
in shower stalls, hidden.

And if it's ICE?

Especially then.

Tamales Mean You've Arrived

No joke
to abuelas
who spend
days wrapping.
Only best teachers
deserve this gift.

WHAT I DON'T EXPECT

Ten thousand dollars they give you. Ten thousand
dollars. —A Raisin in the Sun

Ask students what they would do
if their family suddenly received
windfall like the Youngers. What

they would do. What their mamas
would do. Expect to hear plans
to buy cars, shoes, maybe a house.

Suggest I would save money
for son's college account. Maybe
pay off a bill or book a vacation.

Never occurs to me purchasing food
would be more than one student's answer.

I scramble eggs, cut cantaloupe,
pour orange juice into paper cups,
plug in crockpot to warm gravy they

ladle over biscuits I rise at *morning-*
dark to bake before school because
it doesn't take much to feed my kids

except to know.

Clean Slate

I'm going to fight you. I'm serious. Get away from me.
You're going to what? I reply, hands clenched in anger.

We march to carpool line. She, intent to get to Granny.
Me, intent to get to Granny. Both of us livid with the other.

I request she give her speech. She explodes in return.
I insist. She melts down in such rage, it can't possibly

be about this assignment. But, I'm angry. Frustrated
beautiful girl successfully sabotages herself.

If she spent half the energy on her work she does
on talking back, she'd be on honor roll. Know within

my bones someone is messing with her. Unwilling
to throw up my hands, I continue to charge. Side

by side. Four hands in fists. My face an enraged red.
We reach the double doors and exit building. Face

teacher on carpool duty. She scans line for Granny's
car. I look to my colleague and exhale. Time for me

to retreat. Write referral to result in suspension.
Know I lost the battle. Determined not to lose war,

I wait days after she returns. Give her space
in my classroom. Respect her as a human before I

sit next to her, bump my shoulder against her shoulder
and whisper, *guess you're really my daughter now*

we've had our first fight. Startled, she graces me
with smile in return and quietly nods, our heads bowed.

HER NAME WAS DESTINY

I did not know
her well before
empty seat echoed
her absence, pulled
to new county, back
to her mama, deemed
safe enough to house
fourteen-year-old girl.

I did not know
only moments of peace
she found in fourth bell,
encouraged to be a child
play-acting in Drama
class, wearing wigs, hats,
and the invisibility glasses,
magic trick worn to
overcome stage-fright.

I did not know
where to turn when
my class poured tears
when bell rang to share
she hanged herself night
before. Hanged herself
in her mama's garage.
Hanged herself to escape.

I did not know
her body was traded
object of exchange
for quick hit. Did not
know the state was wrong.
Did not know her empty
seat foreshadowed

Destiny.

CLAW-FOOTED TUB

I pray the silent Buddha and chant sea salts
turn diamond stanzas within bath water I immerse
my seal body until only my face, breasts, and thigh tops
mound exposed to the air causing steam to rise I breathe
deeply my hair cascades around me and my ears remember

the childhood tunnel I had forgotten
in my haste for utilitarian showers in mornings
between cups of coffee and bus tokens
drop as easily into fountains because they fail
to hold any more magic than the common copper
penny that isn't very common anymore. With what
do they make pennies now? When houses

are made of cardboard called drywall and windows
plastic as we walk Formica floors, it is difficult
to trust authenticity stamped and dated by Pottery
Barn and underscored by hip hop versions of remixed
classics dating no later than 1986, which makes me
older than I care to admit as my stomach slick
rises and falls. My bellybutton
holds water like a thimble turned upside down
catching raindrops, only I do not rust. I wonder

how someone my age is already dead and why
I am not and it has become apparent every yellow
rubber duck evidence of sustainability as I use my toe
to pull the chain holding the drain, it must all go somewhere.

She says she lost a son. I cannot share
sympathy great enough to fill the crack
my heart cuts in empathy. I would follow
the swirl without hesitation lost in agony
Edward Munch screams on a bridge

the troll demands his coin and air chills my skin
I use Turkish towels to remind me of cats
in the ancient ruins of Ephesus and mosaic sidewalks
warning *Cave Canem* unnecessary because the hounds
already unleashed in my heart as I howl and bark and growl
until the yellow smoke of Prufrock's city entices
my soul to smoke hookah sitting cross-legged drinking tea
as the women come and go, talking of Michelangelo
when all I really want to do is to escape down penny lanes.

CHEAP IMITATIONS

At least you're not fake, Ms. B. You keep it real.

First, you ask how I could take
your comment so personally.
You, who hides behind a mask
that is just so hideous, and I hate
when people say *irregardless.*
They do not mean with regard,
and don't know any better,
but it bothers me anyway,
just like your insincerity
bothers me, and lukewarm soup,
and pennies that aren't even
copper anymore.
It isn't what you think it is.

There are a few things
that are true to what they say:
Kentucky bourbon, Park Avenue
apartments, rollercoaster rides,
chocolate ice cream cones, daffodils,
library books, cigarettes, and apples.

The rest is unreliable, and I am
learning to temper expectations.
I no longer expect anything,
not even good grammar
because the weather changes
and the moon changes
and the light changes
and I've never held
a fascination for the magician,
not even as a kid.

His shiny, ill-fitting
suit betrayed any authority
his rabbit might have held,

and I don't like cheap shoes.
I would rather pay for expensive,
designer leather because even my feet
recognize imitations.

The Rules

There is a fine line
to balance, choices
to be made against
fate when exercising
free will. You should

not feel guilty. I know
you carry grief. Forever
wonder what if. Small
price to pay, in my mind.
Selfish, my son is alive.

Cost too great when parents
turn away for split-second,
yet who can possibly watch
every moment? Dare fall
asleep and you can lose

your children who sneak
out to—

to be kids, who don't
think. Like when we

were young and stupid,
smoking and drinking,
windows open, hair
flying, music blasting,
laughter yelling chaos.

Only difference,
an inconvenient tree.
A patch of black ice.
Stroke of bad luck.
Two coffins. Wailing

Mother. Stench
of lilies. I recite
the Lord's Prayer
and realize you don't
know the words.

Does it matter
I raised you to pray
in the trees and not
in the church? One
decision after another,

parenting a series
of choices. Where
is that handbook I
received when you
were born? You

know, the one
that tells me what
to do exactly for you.
The one that could
have kept the brothers

alive.

FOR YOU

Before we leave, you check
your hair. Ask if you should
iron your shirt. I say no. Ask
if you sprayed that expensive
cologne. You say yes. We smile.

I don't have to remind you
to shake her mother's hand
on the front porch when you
knock and I wait behind.

October, Sunday afternoon
matinee date of a film you both
read as novel in English class
sitting side-by-side in the backseat

as I drive your fifteen-year-old
selves where you can walk
after to share a pizza, talking
about what, I don't know. I
was never this young. My heart
breaks as I drive away, squinting
in the sunshine.

AND I SO HATE RHYMES

Let your children name themselves
—Saul Williams

I just want
to talk with you
(sirens interrupt
silence abruptly).

And then, soon
as you speak,
(elevator muzak,
grocery aisle
announcements).

You insert
white plugs
into ears
intent more
on beats
and lyrics
that resonate
deep within
your newly
evolving soul
(I so crave to see).

Again, speak
not with fervor,
embarrassing heat,
but instead
with dignity
from your soul
radiating through
your feet.

(And I so hate rhymes
as well as all caps each line.)

But in my haste
to be involved
in your journey,
you withdraw
(as you should).

Punctuation
found within
fire drills at school
must be endured
to prepare me
for you to leave,
(as you should).

Insert parenthesizes
and paragraphs.
Chapters if you
absolutely must.
(And you must).

Divide the line.

Continue culture
only as you
see necessary
to your own
existence or
more importantly,
relevantly,
impossibly,
in what you teach
beyond yourself through
stories to friends,
lessons to students,
anecdotes to protégées,
(which in itself

is such an awkward
term in the era
of tossing around
the word, mentor).

Nonetheless,
stories to protégés
are wonderful
in their honesty
and hyperbolic
humility. Hubris,
a coat worn
in shame.

Name yourself.
(Rename
if necessary).

Echo the moon.
Boomerang
beyond Mars.

Forget astronomy
and question authority
and then pay attention
to the stars.

Summer Blues

Wish I was still
in the classroom
to tack these two
posters on the wall
like this:

you   don't
matter   give up

Mostly because
I miss making
my students laugh
just like I miss

bells, sneakers, pencils, open house, broken sharpeners,
homework, backpacks, markers, cafeteria lines, high-
lighters, lockers, bulletin boards, pizza day, lectures,
prom, stickers, buses, gum, posters, detention, gold stars,
fire drills, crayons, lesson plans, desks, announcements,
hall passes, hoodies, grade books, commencement.

don't   give up
you   matter

Acknowledgments

Grateful acknowledgments to the following for publishing versions of these poems:

"Mother's Day Card" and "His Name was Angel" *I Thought I Heard A Cardinal Sing, Ohio's Appalachian Voices* 2022

"Summer Blues" *Workhorse Anthology* 2022

"Even Years Later" *Appalachian Review* 2021

"Hands Up/Don't Shoot" first appeared in *World Gone Mad* 2021

"I Have No Poem Inside Me" *Maps We Forgot To Bring Anthology* 2020

"I met god at the Speedway today" first appeared in *Summer Tour* 2020

"Claw-footed Tub" first appeared in *Interiors*, Finishing Line Press 2011

About the Author

B. Elizabeth Beck is a poet who writes fiction. She is a hybrid author of seven books. The *Summer Tour Trilogy* includes *Summer Tour* (KDP 2020), *World Gone Mad* (KDP 2021), and *Under the Elm* (KDP 2022). Her books of poetry are *Painted Daydreams: Collection of Ekphrastic Poems* (Accents Publishing 2019), *insignificant* (Evening Street Press 2013), and *Interiors* (Finishing Line Press 2013). She achieved her B.A. in English Literature with a minor in Fine Arts from the University of Cincinnati and her M.Ed. from Xavier University. She is an award-winning English and Art History teacher. During her time at Withrow High School, she founded *The Tracks* literary magazine. She is the proud recipient of an Artist Enrichment Grant through the Kentucky Foundation for Women. She founded The Teen Howl Poetry Series and the award-winning Leestown OUTLOUD Poets. In between, Elizabeth likes to make art, cook, and listen to music.

Visit her online at elizbeck.com
facebook.com/B Elizabeth Beck Author
instagram.com/Elizabeth__Bcck
goodreads.com/B Elizabeth Beck